I0140931

MORTICIANS IN LOVE

Christi Stewart-Brown

BROADWAY PLAY PUBLISHING INC
New York
www.broadwayplaypublishing.com
info@broadwayplaypublishing.com

MORTICIANS IN LOVE
© Copyright 2017 Christi Stewart-Brown

All rights reserved. This work is fully protected under the copyright laws of the United States of America. No part of this publication may be photocopied, reproduced, stored in a retrieval system, or transmitted, in any form or by any means, electronic, mechanical, recording, or otherwise, without the prior permission of the publisher. Additional copies of this play are available from the publisher.

Written permission is required for live performance of any sort. This includes readings, cuttings, scenes, and excerpts. For amateur and stock performances, please contact Broadway Play Publishing Inc. For all other rights please contact the author c/o B P P I.

Cover art by Ingrid Kallick

First edition: September 2017
I S B N: 978-0-88145-731-5

Book design: Marie Donovan
Page make-up: Adobe InDesign
Typeface: Palatino

MORTICIANS IN LOVE premiered at Woolly
Mammoth Theatre in Washington DC on 10 April 1992.
The cast and creative contribuors were:

LYDIA DRURY .... Bernadette Flagler
LIMER .... Carol Monda
ST JOHN HOMEBODY .... James Joseph Gregorio
CHARLIE ....Christopher Lane
MONIKA...Samantha Griffith

Director .... Jennifer Mendenhall
Lighting designer .... Greg Craddick
Original score ....Ron Ursano
Costume designer ....Susan Anderson
Rehearsal stage manager ....James Hardison
Production stage manager .... James Wilder
Assistant stage managers &
    additional dead bodies ....Gary Telles & Holly Twyford

MORTICIANS IN LOVE subsequently opened Off-Broadway at the Perry Street Theatre in April 1995 with the following cast and creative contributors:

LYDIA DRURY .... Bernadette Flagler
LIMER .... Carol Monda
ST JOHN HOMEBODY .... Warren Keith
CHARLIE .... Eric Nolan
MONIKA .... Gabriela May Ladd & Carla Johnston

Director .... Jennifer Mendenhall
Set designer .... Michael McGarty
Lighting designer .... Russell H Champs
Sound design .... One Dream Sound
Costume designer .... Susan Anderson
Stage manager .... Bethany Ford

CHARACTERS & SETTING

LYDIA DRURY, *a mortician, owner of the Eternal Acres Funeral Home*
ST JOHN HOMEBODY, *a mortician*
LIMER, LYDIA's *assistant**
CHARLIE, *a very good-looking dead body*
MONIKA, *a very good-looking dead body*

Time: The present

Setting: The back room of the Eternal Acres Funeral Home

* LIMER's *gender is never specified in the play and the character is referred to as "it". The character can be played by a suitably androgynous male or female actor. The author respectfully requests that directors resist the temptation to model* LIMER *on the* Saturday Night Live *character Pat from "It's Pat".*

ACT ONE

Scene One

(At rise: a woman, LYDIA, *stands alone on the stage She addresses the audience as if they were customers.)*

LYDIA: Here at Eternal Acres your loved one will be in good hands. My hands. These tiny, delicate, white hands. A woman's hands. Taking delicate, loving care of your loved one. These little hands will lay out and process your loved one with the utmost care.

These little hands will gently insert the trocar—a trocar is an object that closely resembles a hypodermic needle, except it's about two feet long and three quarters of an inch in diameter—insert the trocar ever so gently under the rib cage of your loved one and suck out all of the fluids in the body cavity.

Then these hands will gently replace the fluid with a lightly herbal-scented formaldehyde mixture, or "cavity fluid," thus preventing unsightly decay before the date of the funeral. These hands will then imperceptibly stitch the lips together so that there are no last minute surprises at the ceremony.

And even more important than the lips are the eyes. Carefully, gently, these hands will place under the eyelids small, rounded, flesh-colored devices that fit over the eyeball. The eyelids are then pulled down over the device and the serrated surface keeps the eyes firmly shut. It simply wouldn't do to risk the eyes opening during the wake.

And lastly, the gentle, loving, somewhat larger hands of my assistant will dress the body, style the hair, and apply make-up that gives the illusion of life itself.

All this for six thousand, nine hundred, ninety-nine dollars, coffin included.

(Blackout)

Scene Two

(LIMER, an androgynous-looking creature, stands downstage in a spotlight., as if in a doorway It is carrying a silver tea service.)

LIMER: Miss?

(No answer)

LIMER: Are you up, Miss?

(No answer)

LIMER: Breakfast is ready.

(No answer)

LIMER: Hello?

(LIMER looks around, but clearly no one is there. It exits with the tray.)

Scene Three

(The back room. Lights come up on LYDIA , who is asleep with her arm around a young man [CHARLIE], her head is on his chest; they are partially covered by a sheet. He has a prominent erection jutting up under the sheet. Neither one moves for a moment. She stirs sleepily and strokes hiss chest; she sits up, stretches, and smiles at him. He does not move.)

LYDIA: Oh, goodness. Boy, I just passed right out—that was exhausting. My, my, Charlie, you are a big boy— just wore me right out. I mean…that was…that was… something else.

(As LYDIA *speaks, she starts straightening up the sheet and* CHARLIE; *she puts his hands under the sheet, smoothes his hair, closes his mouth, etc…)*

LYDIA: Don't get the wrong idea about me, Charlie, I don't normally do this right after meeting someone… but you were…well, you were just irresistible. Such a lovely body you've got. I so rarely meet such perfect specimens and I am very much looking forward to the time that we will be able to spend together here in my humble abode.

*(*LIMER *enters and stands quietly, waiting to be noticed.)*

LYDIA: You wait, Charlie, tonight I won't be so tired and—

*(*LYDIA *notices* LIMER *and jumps slightly.)*

LYDIA: Limer, please do not sneak in here like that, you know I can't stand it.

LIMER: I beg your pardon, Miss.

LYDIA: What is it?

LIMER: Breakfast is ready, Miss.

LYDIA: Good, I'm starving.

*(*LIMER *stands waiting.)*

LYDIA: Was there something else, Limer?

LIMER: The rats are back, Miss.

LYDIA: Where?

LIMER: Seems they were frolicking about in the embalming room last night. Chewed off one of Mr Franklin's toes.

LYDIA: Anything else?

LIMER: The tip of Mrs Dougherty's finger.

LYDIA: Which finger?

LIMER: Middle finger. Right hand.

LYDIA: Oh, well we'll just cover it with her left hand. Thank heavens it wasn't her ring finger.

LIMER: Yes, Miss.

LYDIA: Any other damage?

LIMER: No, Miss.

LYDIA: Good.

LIMER: Is this a new one, Miss?

LYDIA: nodding

Mac brought him in the middle of the night. Motorcycle accident. Broken neck. Very clean break. Hardly any bruises on the body.

LIMER: Nice, is he?

LYDIA: Take a look.

(LIMER *lifts the sheet and lets out a low whistle.*)

LIMER: Your lucky night.

LYDIA: God was indeed smiling down upon me.

LIMER: Too many old people dying...

LYDIA: Well, that's as it should be...

LIMER: It's the nursing home, Miss.

LYDIA: They keep us in business, Limer.

LIMER: Homebody gets all the young ones.

LYDIA: He's in a better neighborhood—more crime on that side of town.

LIMER: Yes, Miss. (*Pause*) Your breakfast, Miss?

LYDIA: I'll be out in a moment.

LIMER: Yes, Miss.

(LYDIA *crosses to* CHARLIE, *reaches under the sheet and struggles with something for a moment. She pulls out a rod, about eight inches long. His "erection" deflates. She wipes the rod on the sheet and puts it away.* LIMER *enters carrying a small box, it watches her for a moment, before making it's presence known.)*

LIMER: Miss?

LYDIA: Yes?

LIMER: I thought you might want these.

LYDIA: What is it?

LIMER: Cavity fluid samples. Mr Wiggins dropped them by yesterday.

LYDIA: Are we running low?

LIMER: No, Miss. It's just that these are new scents. I thought perhaps you might like one of them for…

LYDIA: Charlie.

LIMER: Charlie.

LYDIA: Are they nice?

LIMER: I believe so. They're perfumes.

LYDIA: Perfumes?

LIMER: Popular perfumes, I believe. Mr. Wiggins says they mask the formaldehyde smell better than the herbal-scented fluid.

(LIMER *holds one out and* LYDIA *smells it.)*

LYDIA: That's nice. What is it?

LIMER: *(Reading the label)* It's called Obsession for Men. There's also Brut, Stetson, and Aramis.

LYDIA: What a lovely idea.

LIMER: I just thought for Charlie, you might want…

LYDIA: How thoughtful, Limer.

LIMER: Yes, Miss.

(LIMER *stands holding the box and looking at* LYDIA *expectantly. She is waiting for it to leave.*)

LYDIA: I'll be out in a moment, Limer.

LIMER: Yes, Miss.

(LIMER *hands the box to* LYDIA *and exits. She takes out a bottle and smells it. She dabs some on* CHARLIE.)

LYDIA: Mmm, doesn't that smell good, Charlie? Very manly. (*She kisses him.*) Now if you'll excuse me, I'm off to have some breakfast and put the finishing touches on Mr. Franklin. And then your parents are coming to see me, isn't that exciting? Don't worry, I won't let them see you like this. Busy day ahead at Eternal Acres, yes siree. (*She pulls the sheet over his head and exits.*)

(*Blackout*)

Scene Four

(*A man,* ST JOHN HOMEBODY, *enters, looking for* LYDIA. *There are a couple more bodies in the room in addition to* CHARLIE. ST JOHN *looks around at the bodies, looking under the sheets, etc... When he gets to* CHARLIE *he lets out a low whistle.*)

ST JOHN: Nice. Very nice.

(LYDIA *enters. And comes up noiselessly behind* ST JOHN.)

LYDIA: Mr Homebody?

ST JOHN: Oh, I'm sorry—I didn't hear you come in. Miss Drury, I presume?

(ST JOHN *extends his hand and they do a "dead fish" handshake.*)

LYDIA: Lydia. So nice to finally meet you, Saint John.
I've read about your work in the obituaries.

ST JOHN: Sinjun.

LYDIA: Pardon?

ST JOHN: My name. It's pronounced Sinjun.

LYDIA: I see. Did Limer send you back here? You could
have waited out front.

ST JOHN: There was a family there.

LYDIA: Charlie's parents.

ST JOHN: Which one is Charlie?

(LYDIA *points.*)

ST JOHN: Oh. They must be very upset.

(*Pause,* LYDIA *and* ST JOHN *both look admiringly at*
CHARLIE.)

LYDIA: So—Sinjun—what brings you to this part of
town?

ST JOHN: The fire.

LYDIA: The fire.

ST JOHN: Horrible.

LYDIA: Fire is horrible.

ST JOHN: Frightening.

LYDIA: Any fire in particular?

ST JOHN: My fire!

LYDIA: Your fire.

ST JOHN: At the mortuary.

LYDIA: I see. There was a fire at your mortuary?

ST JOHN: Night before last. You hadn't heard?

LYDIA: No.

ST JOHN: It was on the news.

LYDIA: I'm afraid I don't watch much television.

ST JOHN: The building was badly burned. They think it was arson.

LYDIA: Goodness, who would want to burn down a mortuary?

ST JOHN: Local ruffians, I'm sure. It's a bad neighborhood.

LYDIA: Good business, though, I would imagine.

ST JOHN: We do a brisk trade, I'll admit.

LYDIA: Completely destroyed, was it?

ST JOHN: No, not completely. Insurance will cover repairs, but it'll be a couple of months before they're completed.

LYDIA: People are afraid of us.

ST JOHN: Excuse me?

LYDIA: People. They're afraid of us. They get nervous around us. They get hostile. Burn things down.

ST JOHN: It's a perfectly respectable profession. I don't understand the fuss people make.

LYDIA: The jokes.

ST JOHN: The jokes are the worst.

LYDIA: I don't go out anymore. Can't stand the jokes.

ST JOHN: Me neither.

LYDIA: Anyway, the fire…

ST JOHN: Well, the thing is—I don't have anywhere to work at the moment, you know, until the repairs are finished, and I thought you might be able to sort of hire me temporarily.

LYDIA: I see.

ST JOHN: You see, if I'm working here, all of my customers will come here—and since my place is out of commission because of the fire, you'll have more business than you can handle, so I thought we could just sort of team up for a while.

LYDIA: I don't know…I'm not really used to working with anybody.

ST JOHN: I hear it's going to be a bad winter.

LYDIA: Really?

ST JOHN: They're expecting the flu to kill off hundreds.

LYDIA: I hadn't heard.

ST JOHN: And New Year's Eve. You know how crazy that gets.

LYDIA: Busiest night of the year, next to Labor Day.

ST JOHN: Anyway, I would ask you to think about it. I have no other source of income, you see, and I certainly don't want to end up here this winter—on the table I mean—like poor Charlie here.

(LYDIA *takes a quick inventory of his body.*)

ST JOHN: Mind you, this would be a nice place to be under those circumstances, but—

LYDIA: I shall think about it and let you know.

ST JOHN: Thank you very much, Miss Drury.

LYDIA: Lydia, please.

ST JOHN: Thank you, Lydia. Good day.

LYDIA: Good day, St John.

(ST JOHN *exits.* LYDIA *goes to* CHARLIE.)

LYDIA: What do you think, Charlie? Shall we give the poor saint a job? Hm?

(LIMER *enters silently,* LYDIA *jumps slightly when she notices it.*)

Jesus, Mary and Joseph, Limer!

LIMER: Beg pardon, Miss.

LYDIA: What is it?

LIMER: Telephone, Miss. City morgue. More bodies.

LYDIA: Where on earth are we going to put all these bodies? They've already sent over two today.

LIMER: It's the fire, Miss.

LYDIA: I suppose so.

LIMER: Homebody's out of business for a while.

LYDIA: Yes, yes, I know.

LIMER: We'll be getting more business now.

LYDIA: We've already got enough business.

LIMER: Better selection this way, Miss.

LYDIA: St John's going to have to help me with this.

LIMER: Sinjun, Miss?

LYDIA: Homebody. He wants to work here with us until the repairs on his place are completed.

LIMER: Will you allow that, Miss?

LYDIA: I don't have much choice.

LIMER: I can help you, Miss. We don't need Homebody.

LYDIA: You're not licensed.

LIMER: I'm a licensed beautician.

LYDIA: Limer…

LIMER: I know the process—I've seen it enough times. No one need know.

LYDIA: I can't risk that.

LIMER: I could work in the middle of the night—

LYDIA: No, Limer.

LIMER: No, Limer.

LYDIA: What?

LIMER: Nothing.

LYDIA: Call St John, Limer. Tell him to come back as soon as possible.

LIMER: If you're sure, Miss…

LYDIA: I'm sure.

LIMER: As you wish.

(LIMER *exits.* LYDIA *covers* CHARLIE, *then takes a look at one of the other bodies. She raises her eyebrows.)*

LYDIA: Closed casket for you, my friend.

(LYDIA *looks at the third body. It's a young woman. She smiles, touches the body, strokes the hair.)*

LYDIA: Goodness. What's your name, dear?

(LYDIA *lifts the sheet over the body's feet and checks the toe tag.* LIMER *enters.)*

LYDIA: Monika. Mon-i-ka. Mohhhneeeka! Nice to meet you, Monika. Charlie, this is Monika. Perhaps the sometime the three of us could—

LIMER: Beg pardon, Miss.

LYDIA: What is it?

LIMER: I left a message for Mr Homebody, Miss.

LYDIA: Thank you, Limer. Anything else?

LIMER: Mac has taken Mr Franklin to the church. There's a free table in the embalming room…

LYDIA: Right. Well, let's get Charlie in there—first come, first served.

LIMER: Exactly, Miss.

(LIMER *and* LYDIA *wheel* CHARLIE *off stage.)*

(Blackout)

Scene Five

(Later that day. St John *enters.)*

St John: Hello? Anybody here? Lydia? Limer?

*(*St John *stands waiting for a moment, then pokes around under the sheets, looking at the bodies. He gets to the third body and pulls back the sheet—it is* Lydia, *asleep.)*

St John: Aaaaaagh!

Lydia: *(Clutching the sheet)* Aaaaaagh! What the hell are you doing?

St John: *(Clutching his hear)* Oh-mi-God, oh-mi-God, oh-mi-God!

Lydia: You nearly scared me to death!

St John: Me?! What are you doing under there?

Lydia: Taking a nap, what does it look like? What are you doing creeping around in here?

St John: I got a message from Limer. It said to come over and help.

*(*Limer *enters.)*

Limer: Everything all right in here?

St John: Everything's fine, Limer. May I have a glass of water please?

Limer: Certainly, sir. There's a sink in the embalming room.

St John: Oh. Okay. *(He exits.)*

Limer: Did you have a nice nap, Miss?

Lydia: Not particularly.

Limer: Very sorry to hear that, Miss. *(Pause. It looks as if it wants to say something.)*

Lydia: Is there something you needed, Limer?

LIMER: Might I make a suggestion on a sensitive topic, Miss?

LYDIA: Go ahead.

LIMER: It's Charlie, Miss.

LYDIA: What about him?

LIMER: It's his mouth, Miss.

LYDIA: Yes?

LIMER: Well, Miss. It seems when you stitched his lips, you—perhaps inadvertently—stitched a smile on them.

LYDIA: He's smiling?

LIMER: Just a little. I think it might upset the relatives to see him so happy while they're feeling quite miserable.

LYDIA: Yes, you're right. I wasn't aware I'd done that.

LIMER: Easy mistake.

LYDIA: Thank you, Limer. Thank you for bringing that to my attention.

LIMER: I take good care of you, do I not?

LYDIA: You do.

LIMER: You're welcome.

LYDIA: Thank you.

LIMER: Shall I take another body into the embalming room, Miss?

LYDIA: Take that one, he'll be closed casket—easy job. I'll give it to St John.

LIMER: Naturally. Save your own talents for Monika.

LYDIA: Mmm. Yes. Monika.

(ST JOHN enters.)

LIMER: Feeling better, sir?

ST JOHN: I'm fine.

LIMER: Glad to hear it, sir. *(It starts to exit.)*

LYDIA: Limer?

LIMER: Yes, Miss?

LYDIA: Why don't you bring Charlie in and I'll finish him in here, then we can get Monika into the embalming room with Mr Closed Casket.

LIMER: As you wish, Miss.

(LIMER exits. ST JOHN watches it go.)

ST JOHN: How long has Limer worked for you?

LYDIA: Oh, for ages.

ST JOHN: May I ask you a question?

LYDIA: Certainly.

ST JOHN: What exactly is Limer?

LYDIA: A licensed beautician.

ST JOHN: I mean what gender is Limer?

LYDIA: Heavens, I've never thought to ask.

ST JOHN: Then what pronoun do you use when referring to Limer?

LYDIA: It.

ST JOHN: It?

LYDIA: It. It just felt natural to do so. I did it without thinking.

ST JOHN: And it—Limer—doesn't mind?

LYDIA: Well, it's never said anything.

ST JOHN: I see.

LYDIA: I could ask it if you like.

ST JOHN: No, no. That's okay. I was just curious.

(LIMER wheels CHARLIE in.)

LYDIA: Hello, Charlie.

ST JOHN: Afternoon, Charlie.

(LIMER *wheels out "Mr Closed Casket".*)

LYDIA: You can start with him, if you like. Closed casket.

ST JOHN: Of course.

LYDIA: Easy job.

ST JOHN: Listen, Lydia—I very much appreciate you sharing your shop with me like this. I don't know what I would have done.

LYDIA: Well, we morticians have to look out for one another. People can be so cruel.

ST JOHN: Especially to a mortician out of work. Doesn't make sense if you think about.

LYDIA: Exactly. And I couldn't just throw you to the worms, now, could I?

ST JOHN: Wolves.

LYDIA: Wolves. And besides, business is already picking up because of the fire.

ST JOHN: Yes, I'm sure.

LYDIA: It's a steady enough business without adding someone else's bodies to it.

ST JOHN: It's a good business.

LYDIA: You come from a family of morticians, do you?

ST JOHN: Naturally. You?

LYDIA: Naturally. This was my mother's place until she died.

ST JOHN: Mine was my father's until he died.

LYDIA: Yes, I remember your father.

ST JOHN: You met him?

LYDIA: Just his body.

ST JOHN: Oh, right. Mother sent the body here. I wanted to do it, but she wouldn't allow it.

LYDIA: It's not a good idea.

ST JOHN: Wait. Your mother…we did your mother.

LYDIA: Quite right.

ST JOHN: So we're acquainted on some level already.

(LYDIA *and* ST JOHN *look over one another's bodies.*)

LYDIA: You resemble your father.

ST JOHN: And you your mother. She was a fine looking lady for her age.

LYDIA: She was only fifty when she died.

ST JOHN: She looked thirty.

LYDIA: Your father, too, was remarkably well-preserved for his age.

ST JOHN: He ran a mile around the cemetery every day until he died.

LYDIA: A tradition you carry on?

ST JOHN: Naturally. I loved my father.

LYDIA: Me too. My mother I mean. *(Quickly)* Well, there's lots to do—shall we get started?

ST JOHN: Certainly. I'll just go and wash up, then get started on Mr Closed Casket.

LYDIA: Very well.

ST JOHN: Shall I start on the girl after that?

LYDIA: No, I'll take care of Monika. There are some bodies coming in from the morgue, you can start on them when they arrive.

ST JOHN: Right.

LYDIA: I'll be in to join you in a moment, I just have to finish stitching Charlie.

ST JOHN: Okay.

LYDIA: Limer will help you find things.

ST JOHN: Thank you, Lydia. You're most kind.

(ST JOHN *attempts a sort of smile towards* LYDIA, *which she attempts to return. It's more eerie than cheery. He exits. She uncovers* CHARLIE's *face, he is smiling too.*)

LYDIA: Now there's a beautiful smile. Hello, Charlie. Did you miss me? I certainly missed you. I'm sorry, but the smile will have to come off. Pity—it suits you. I bet you smiled a lot. I don't know how to smile very well. Smiles are rarely called for in this business. Just one kiss before that beautiful face stops smiling.

(LYDIA *kisses* CHARLIE *on the lips lightly, then again more fervently.* LIMER *enters with a tray on which are scissors, needles, black thread and a sandwich.* LYDIA *kisses* CHARLIE *once more then yelps. She straightens up, hand covering her mouth.*)

LYDIA: Forgot about the stitches, didn't I Charlie?

LIMER: I don't have stitches, Miss.

LYDIA: *(Slightly startled)* Pardon?

LIMER: I brought some stitching material for Charlie. And a sandwich for you, Miss.

LYDIA: Why thank you, Limer. That was very thoughtful.

LIMER: You're welcome.

LYDIA: How is St John getting on in there?

(LYDIA *picks up the scissors and snips the stitches out of* CHARLIE's *lips with one hand, she eats her sandwich with the other.*)

LIMER: Splendidly, Miss.

LYDIA: Lovely sandwich, Limer.

LIMER: You're welcome.

LYDIA: Is St John finding everything all right? *(She pulls some black thread out of* CHARLIE's *mouth.)*

LIMER: He is as happy as a pig in mud, Miss. Shall I thread your needle for you, Miss?

LYDIA: Thank you, Limer. That would be very nice.

LIMER: I don't need a license to thread needles, do I?

LYDIA: Don't be angry with me, Limer. Rules are rules. I'm not a law-breaker.

LIMER: Yes, Miss. The family brought Charlie's burial suit, Miss. Shall I dress him after you're done?

LYDIA: No, I don't think so, Limer. Charlie isn't to be buried for a couple of days—we'll dress him Saturday morning.

LIMER: As you wish, Miss. I'll go do Monika's nails. She's wearing a most inappropriate shade of red on her fingernails. A whore, no doubt.

LYDIA: Limer! Judge not, lest ye be judged.

LIMER: Yes, Miss.

LYDIA: We're closer to God because of our jobs, but we mustn't play God. We just make sure people look good when they go to meet God.

LIMER: Yes, Miss.

LYDIA: Now run along, Limer and let me finish up Charlie.

LIMER: Run along, Limer.

LYDIA: What?

LIMER: Nothing.

*(*LIMER *plunks the threaded needle down on* CHARLIE's *chest and exits.* LYDIA *rearranges* CHARLIE's *mouth. She tries several expressions, until she finds one she likes.)*

LYDIA: There. That should be suitably somber. You look very rugged and handsome in that expression, Charlie.

(LYDIA *leans over and kisses him, rearranges his mouth, then starts stitching. After a moment,* ST JOHN *pokes his head in; he holds a bottle in his hand.*)

ST JOHN: Excuse me, Lydia…

LYDIA: Yes?

ST JOHN: I can't find a bucket to mix the cavity fluid in.

LYDIA: Oh, heavens, St John, you don't have to do that. Have Limer do it.

ST JOHN: I don't mind. Really. (*He looks over her shoulder at* CHARLIE.) You do nice work.

LYDIA: Thank you.

ST JOHN: I'm glad to see you still stitch lips. Most people use that horrible glue these days.

LYDIA: Terrible stuff. I can't stand it.

ST JOHN: I preferred it when he was smiling, though.

LYDIA: Oh. Silly me. I don't know what I was thinking when I did that.

ST JOHN: Sometimes it's nice to see them smile.

LYDIA: You would think the families would want to see one last smile and remember their loved ones like that. Smiling.

(*Pause*)

ST JOHN: Lydia?

LYDIA: Yes?

ST JOHN: I was wondering if you might perhaps care to have dinner with me this evening…

LYDIA: Dinner?

ST JOHN: Just to, you know, talk over business, you know, just come to some agreement for the time we'll be working together.

LYDIA: You mean go out?

ST JOHN: Well, yes.

LYDIA: To a restaurant?

ST JOHN: Yes, I suppose so.

LYDIA: I don't like going out to restaurants. People stare...

(LIMER enters.)

ST JOHN: Maybe dinner isn't a good idea.

LYDIA: We could have dinner here. Limer is a wonderful cook, aren't you Limer?

LIMER: Superb.

ST JOHN: That would be lovely.

LYDIA: *(She glances at CHARLIE.)* But not tonight. This has been such a long day. Saturday perhaps.

ST JOHN: Saturday is fine.

LYDIA: Would that be okay with you, Limer?

LIMER: I can think of nothing I'd rather do, Miss...

LYDIA: Good.

LIMER: Except perhaps to shave my entire body with a dull razor.

LYDIA: What?

LIMER: Nothing. *(It exits.)*

ST JOHN: I think something's bothering it.

LYDIA: Limer? Don't be silly. It's as happy as a pig in mud.

(Blackout)

Scene Six

(Lights up to dim. LIMER *sits buffing* MONIKA*'s nails. It sings the* Dwarf Song *from* Snow White and the Seven Dwarfs*.)*

LIMER: Hi ho, hi ho
It's off to work we go
We clean the dead
Then go to bed
Hi ho, hi ho, hi ho

Hi ho, Hi ho
It's in the ground you go
You've had your turn
Now feed the worms
Hi hi, Hi ho, Hi ho

*(*LYDIA *enters, she is dressed in night clothes.)*

LYDIA: Oh, it's you. I thought I heard singing.

LIMER: The Dwarf Song, Miss.

LYDIA: Oh.

LIMER: My parents were dwarfs.

LYDIA: I see. What did your parents do?

LIMER: Grave diggers, Miss.

LYDIA: Really? That's exciting.

LIMER: Not like here. It wasn't much fun unless they let me help spread lime on the bodies.

LYDIA: You mean they didn't embalm the bodies?

LIMER: No need, Miss. Lime keeps the smell down long enough to get them buried.

LYDIA: Where do you come from anyway?

LIMER: A long, long way away. You won't have heard of it.

LYDIA: It's extremely unsanitary not to embalm the dead.

LIMER: Some people don't think it necessary.

LYDIA: Well it is. Lime! That's barbaric.

LIMER: *(Getting defensive now)* Well, I suppose it just depends on what's important to you.

LYDIA: And what's important to you, Limer?

LIMER: This place. You.

LYDIA: That's very sweet of you. You're the most dedicated employee I've ever had. Most can't take it very long.

LIMER: They're just bodies. They can't hurt you. Can't feel anything.

LYDIA: Mmm.

LIMER: I'm sorry I said what I said about Monika today. I'm sure she was a nice girl.

LYDIA: It's okay.

LIMER: *(Holding up one of* MONIKA's *hands.)* Look. Hands of a nun. Wouldn't want her family seeing her in that frightful red—got to let parents have their illusions about their children.

LYDIA: Of course.

LIMER: Well, Miss. I think I'll go turn in.

LYDIA: All right.

LIMER: Would you like me to read you to sleep, Miss?

LYDIA: No, thank you. I'm fine.

LIMER: Some warm milk, perhaps?

LYDIA: I'm fine, Limer.

LIMER: Yes, Miss. *(Pause)* Miss, I…

LYDIA: Yes?

LIMER: Nothing. Goodnight, Miss.

LYDIA: Goodnight, Limer. Sleep well.

(LIMER *exits.* LYDIA *listens until she can't hear it anymore, then goes over to* MONIKA. *She lifts the sheet and squeals delightedly. She pulls the sheet farther down to reveal* MONIKA *dressed in sexy lingerie.* LYDIA *strokes the fabric.*)

LYDIA: Oooo, how beautiful you look. Now wasn't that thoughtful of Limer? Mmm, such soft fabric.

(LYDIA *kisses* MONIKA, *then goes to* CHARLIE *and pulls the sheet off—he has also been dressed in sexy underwear.*)

LYDIA: Oooo Charlie, you sly devil! Look what he's got on, Monika! Let's go over and visit with Monika, shall we?

(LYDIA *wheels* CHARLIE'*s gurney over to* MONIKA'*s, making a "double bed" out of the two gurneys.*)

LYDIA: Oh gosh, I've never had a threesome before— I'm so nervous. Let's take this slowly, shall we?

(LYDIA*e pulls* MONIKA *into a sitting position and puts* MONIKA'*s arms around herself.*)

LYDIA: Oh heavens, you're beautiful.

(LYDIA *kisses* MONIKA. MONIKA'*s eyes fly open.*)

LYDIA: Oh dear! Forgot your eye discs, didn't I? Oh well.

(LYDIA *kisses* MONIKA *again.*)

(*Blackout*)

Scene Seven

(*The lights come up on the bodies lying in their double gurney. In between* CHARLIE *and* MONIKA *there is another body under the sheet.* CHARLIE *has an "erection."* LIMER *enters quietly and peeks under the sheet. It smiles slightly. It*

hears something and steps back to watch the inevitable scene.
LYDIA *enters and then stops abruptly upon seeing a third*
body on the gurneys. She does not see LIMER *in the shadows.*
She pulls back the sheet to reveal ST JOHN, *asleep between*
CHARLIE *and* MONIKA.)

LYDIA: St John!

ST JOHN: *(Jolting awake)* What? What time is it? Am I
late for work?

LIMER: It appears you're early, sir.

LYDIA: Limer! Perhaps you could leave us alone for a
moment?

LIMER: But, Miss, I—

LYDIA: Leave, Limer!

LIMER: Yes, Miss. *(It exits.)*

LYDIA: St John, might I ask what in heavens name you
are doing here?

ST JOHN: I couldn't sleep.

LYDIA: So you came here to…to…

ST JOHN: I didn't think you'd mind.

LYDIA: Might I remind you that this is my mortuary
and these are my bodies.

ST JOHN: Well, I thought they were ours—for the time
being anyway.

LYDIA: You've no right to them.

ST JOHN: But they would've been mine if it weren't for
the fire. They're from my neighborhood.

*(*LYDIA *suddenly spots* CHARLIE's *erection. She reaches*
under the sheet and pulls out her contraption.)

LYDIA: And this! This is my personal invention!

ST JOHN: It's ingenious.

LYDIA: Look, St John, I think we have to get some ground rules straightened out here. This is *my* mortuary, these are *my* bodies, and this is *my* invention. You simply can't just come in here and use whatever you like without my permission. This is highly upsetting.

ST JOHN: I'm very sorry, Lydia. I wasn't thinking.

LYDIA: How would you feel if I just walked into your place and took the best you had for myself?

ST JOHN: You're right. It was very thoughtless of me.

LYDIA: I feel violated, St John. Like I've been...been... been...violated.

ST JOHN: I'm sorry, Lydia. It won't happen again, I promise.

LYDIA: I should certainly hope not.

ST JOHN: It won't.

LYDIA: Get cleaned up and get to work. Monika's family will be arriving shortly.

ST JOHN: Yes, of course.

(LYDIA *exits.* ST JOHN *gets up and starts putting on his suit.* LIMER *enters.*)

LIMER: Would you like some help, sir?

ST JOHN: I think I can manage.

LIMER: I meant with the bodies. They're a bit mussed up. Can't leave them like that. Never know when one of those nasty health inspectors is going to pop in.

ST JOHN: Oh. Yes, thank you, Limer. I'll take care of Charlie, if you'll get Monika.

LIMER: As you wish, sir.

(LIMER *wheels* CHARLIE *away from* MONIKA, *then starts straightening her up, combing her hair, fixing her smile, etc. When* St John *has finished dressing, he starts on* Charlie.*)*

Limer: Nice evening, sir?

St John: Let's not talk about it, Limer.

Limer: No need to be embarrassed.

St John: I'm just saying that I would rather not talk about it.

Limer: Certainly, sir.

(Pause)

St John: Limer?

Limer: Sir?

St John: Does Lydia have a…well, a…boyfriend?

Limer: You mean alive, sir?

St John: Yes, of course.

Limer: No, sir.

St John: Has she ever?

Limer: I don't believe so, sir.

St John: I see.

Limer: I wouldn't hold out much hope, sir.

St John: What do you mean?

Limer: I mean don't get any ideas in your head about Miss Lydia. You're not her type.

St John: How do you know?

Limer: No one is, sir.

St John: I think that's up to her to decide.

Limer: Not necessarily.

St John: What?

Limer: I think it would be futile to try to win Miss Lydia's affections, sir.

ST JOHN: We'll see.

LIMER: Yes.

ST JOHN: You don't like me, do you Limer?

LIMER: No, sir.

ST JOHN: Why not?

LIMER: You're an intruder, sir.

ST JOHN: You'll need the help until my place is repaired.

LIMER: We could manage.

ST JOHN: Perhaps. Perhaps not.

(LIMER *pulls the sheet over* MONIKA*'s head.*)

LIMER: There's an old couple, the Willoughbys, in the embalming room. Double suicide. Miss Lydia said you should work on them today. They should be safe from your... "violations" is the word, I believe.

ST JOHN: Now, wait just a minute—

LIMER: *(Exiting)* I'll be doing Mrs. Willoughby's wig if you need anything.

(ST JOHN *finishes up* CHARLIE. LYDIA *enters.*)

LYDIA: Almost finished?

ST JOHN: I'm done.

LYDIA: There's an old couple in the—

ST JOHN: The Willoughbys, yes I know.

LYDIA: Good. *(She turns to exit.)*

ST JOHN: Lydia?

LYDIA: St John?

(LIMER *enters.*)

ST JOHN: Do we still have a date for tomorrow?

LYDIA: Well, I don't know if that's—

ST JOHN: Please?

LYDIA: All right. *(She exits without seeing* LIMER.*)*

LIMER: It won't work.

ST JOHN: Why not?

LIMER: She doesn't understand the world of the living.

ST JOHN: Neither do I.

LIMER: You've adapted better.

ST JOHN: Butt out, Limer.

(ST JOHN exits. LIMER *stands for a moment. It wipes away a tear, then exits.)*

(Blackout)

Scene Eight

(Saturday morning. CHARLIE *and* MONIKA *are gone. There is one gurney with a body under a sheet.* LYDIA *enters wheeling a second gurney with a body on it.)*

LYDIA: All right, Mr and Mrs Willoughby, you should be very comfortable in here. Together in life, together in death. Very sweet. I wish you could've met Charlie and Monika—they were young and beautiful— perhaps they looked like you when you were young. Perhaps they would've met and married... *(She sniffs.)* I miss them terribly. Oh dear, I must be getting soft. I never cry.

LIMER: *(Entering)* Are you in here, Miss?

LYDIA: Yes.

LIMER: The Willoughby's son is here. He's changed his mind about the coffins. He wants to pick out something else.

LYDIA: But the ones he picked are beautiful. There's enough mahogany in them to make a dining room set.

LIMER: Too expensive. He just found out the estate is smaller than expected. Says he can't afford the mahogany.

LYDIA: What does he want to change to?

LIMER: The aluminum ones.

LYDIA: Aluminum?! An only son wants to bury his only parents in aluminum?!

LIMER: Yes, Miss. Did you want to speak to him?

LYDIA: Let St John talk to him.

LIMER: I thought Homebody was here to help with the bodies, not the grievers.

LYDIA: Please just do as I ask, Limer.

LIMER: I didn't mean to question your judgment, Miss.

LYDIA: I know. Look, Limer, I'm kind of upset right now and I don't feel like talking to anyone. Okay?

LIMER: Yes, Miss. Anything I can do?

LYDIA: Just go get St John and have him talk to Willoughby.

LIMER: Yes, Miss. *(It exits.)*

LYDIA: I'm sorry you had to hear that Mr and Mrs Willoughby. I'm sure your son doesn't mean anything personal by switching the coffins. This often happens when your wishes aren't made clear in the will, or you don't buy your coffins early. "Buy before you die" I always say. That way when your ungrateful children get a hold of your money you are at least assured of a proper home for your eternal rest. *(She suddenly notices something lying on the floor. She picks it up. It is part of a finger, somewhat chewed up.)* Oh dear. Is this…? Oh no! I'd know this finger anywhere! This is Charlie's! Oh

dear God. Oh, I can't stand it! Those goddamned rats!
Why Charlie, why'd they have to pick on Charlie? Why
would they want to maim a perfectly perfect body?
This is too much.

(LYDIA *sobs.* LIMER *enters and sees her crying. It goes up to
her and is about to reach out to her, when it hears* ST JOHN
coming. It exits quickly.)

ST JOHN: Lydia, Willoughby wants to know if—good
heavens, Lydia, what's the matter?

(LYDIA *holds up the finger and waves it without looking at*
ST JOHN.)

ST JOHN: Is that Charlie's?

(LYDIA *nods.)*

ST JOHN: Can't Limer do something about those rats?
It's really quite ghastly the way they scurry around
here at night. Are you all right?

LYDIA: I'm not having a good day.

ST JOHN: Is it Charlie and Monika?

(LYDIA *nods.)*

ST JOHN: Well, the family had to take them eventually.
Not much sense in having a funeral without a body.
That'd be pointless, wouldn't it?

LYDIA: Don't try to cheer me up.

ST JOHN: Is it always this hard on you?

LYDIA: Of course not! Don't you even think I do this
all the time. Just because I'm a woman doesn't mean I
can't handle this job.

ST JOHN: That's not what I meant. Not at all.

LYDIA: If you think jokes about morticians are awful,
you should hear the ones about women morticians.

ST JOHN: I'd rather not.

(ST JOHN *goes to* LYDIA *and puts his arm around her. She leans her head on his chest.*)

ST JOHN: It'll be all right. Sometimes it gets rough, but it never lasts for long. There'll be other Charlies and Monikas. I know that doesn't help right now, but you'll be okay soon. And if you ever want to talk about, you know—things—you just call me, okay?

LYDIA: Thank you, St John. That's very kind.

(LYDIA *and* ST JOHN *look into each other's eyes for a long while. They lean toward each other for a kiss, but as soon as their lips meet they both pull back—they've never kissed living flesh and the movement frightens them.*)

ST JOHN: Oh…

LYDIA: Sorry.

ST JOHN: No, I…sorry.

LYDIA: I… just…

ST JOHN: Yes, well I should get back to the Willoughby boy.

LYDIA: Yes, he'll be getting impatient.

ST JOHN: Oh, he wanted to know if he could get a larger coffin and squeeze them both in.

LYDIA: Absolutely not.

ST JOHN: That's what I told him, but I thought I'd double check.

LYDIA: That man should be buried alive.

(LIMER *enters silently.*)

ST JOHN: Yes. Well, um, I'll go and tell him. See you later.

LYDIA: Dinner tonight?

ST JOHN: Eight o'clock.

(ST JOHN *turns and almost bumps into* LIMER. *He exits.*)

ST JOHN: Jesus Christ, Limer! *(He exits.)*

LYDIA: Did you need something, Limer?

LIMER: No.

LYDIA: *(She holds up* CHARLIE's *finger.)* The rats are at it again.

LIMER: Is that Charlie's?

LYDIA: Yes.

LIMER: Oh, dear, I'm so sorry. That must be very upsetting for you.

LYDIA: It is. Isn't there anything you can do about them?

LIMER: I'm doing my best to get rid of them, Miss. I can't do more than that, can I?

LYDIA: I'm sorry, I didn't mean to snap at you.

LIMER: After all, I'm a beautician, not a trained rat killer.

LYDIA: I'm sorry.

LIMER: Apology accepted. *(It turns to exit.)*

LYDIA: Limer?

LIMER: Miss?

LYDIA: Is anything the matter?

LIMER: What do you mean?

LYDIA: You seem out of sorts lately.

LIMER: I'm fine, Miss.

LYDIA: Good. Um…dinner tonight?

LIMER: It will be ready at eight, Miss.

*(*LIMER *exits.* LYDIA *gets out a little jar of formaldehyde and drops* CHARLIE's *finger into it.)*

LYDIA: Well, Charlie, I guess I'll just have to be satisfied with having a little piece of you.

END OF ACT ONE

ACT TWO

Scene One

(*At rise,* LIMER *is clearing dishes from* LYDIA*'s and* ST JOHN*'s date. One of the gurneys serves as a table. It's covered with a table cloth, there are flowers on it and two candles.*)

ST JOHN: Eventually, though, the crematoriums are going to put us out of business. Land is too valuable to be using for the dead.

LYDIA: They won't put us out of business, we'll just have to change with the times.

ST JOHN: I don't know, Lydia, maybe I'm old-fashioned, but give me a graveside ceremony. This scattering of ashes and these memorial services without a body just don't work for me.

LYDIA: Well, I agree with you—families certainly cope much better when they see the actual body going into the ground.

ST JOHN: Well, that's exactly it, isn't it? Even though viewing a dead body might seem horrific to these new age types, psychologists agree that it's one way the living start to cope with their grief.

LYDIA: They have to start letting go when they see the body.

ST JOHN: Exactly. I mean ashes...how do you grieve over ashes? They could be from someone's fireplace—how do you even know it's the right body?

LYDIA: It's a problem.

ST JOHN: And the families miss that moment...that wonderful moment when the coffin is slowly lowered into the ground and that first gentle thud of dirt clods strikes the box. That's is such a beautiful, symbolic thing.

LYDIA: You're very passionate about your work, St John.

ST JOHN: Yes, Lydia, I am.

LYDIA: I like that.

ST JOHN: You do? Isn't doesn't embarrass you?

LYDIA: On the contrary, it...it...

ST JOHN: Yes?

LYDIA: I don't know. I don't really have the words for it...

ST JOHN: I understand.

LYDIA: Anyway, St John, despite how we feel about our work, cremation is the wave of the future. We'll have to switch over some day—or at least add the option. In fact, I've thought about adding a crematorium to this place.

ST JOHN: Lydia!

LYDIA: Oh, just a small one. Heavens, St John, don't look at me as if I were some sort of traitor.

ST JOHN: I'm sorry. I just never pictured you as the crematoria type.

LYDIA: Well, I'm not. But I'm not stupid either. I don't want to go out of business just because I prefer a good old-fashioned funeral to the ashes-scattering-bell-ringing-crystal-thing. I'll still try to talk people into going the normal route, but I'd like to give them options.

(LIMER *enters.*)

ST JOHN: You're so sensible.

LIMER: Dessert?

LYDIA: None for me. How about you, St John?

ST JOHN: Thanks, no, Limer. Dinner was wonderful.

LIMER: I'm glad you enjoyed it, sir.

LYDIA: And the room looks wonderful, Limer.

LIMER: You're welcome.

LYDIA: Thank you.

LIMER: Are you sure you wouldn't like some dessert?

LYDIA: I couldn't eat another bite.

LIMER: Not even a slice of birthday cake?

LYDIA: Oh dear. Is it your birthday, Limer? Did I forget it again?

LIMER: It's your birthday, Miss.

LYDIA: Today?

LIMER: Tomorrow, Miss.

ST JOHN: Well, happy birthday, Lydia!

LYDIA: Heavens, I hadn't realized. I never can remember birthdays for some reason.

LIMER: So you'll have some cake, Miss?

LYDIA: Why don't we save it until tomorrow. Since tomorrow's the birthday.

LIMER: I just thought this might be a more special time, seeing as it's your first date and all—

LYDIA: Save it, Limer!

LIMER: Yes, Miss. *(It exits with the last of the dishes.)*

LYDIA: It means well, poor dear, but sometimes it embarrasses me unintentionally.

ST JOHN: Is it true?

LYDIA: No. This is not my first date.

ST JOHN: Oh.

LYDIA: I've had exactly two dates in my entire life. Both disastrous.

ST JOHN: What happened?

LYDIA: Nothing really, which I suppose was the problem. I just couldn't think of anything to say to them. I'm not very good with people.

ST JOHN: I know what you mean. But look, Lydia—we've been talking for hours and it's been absolutely delightful.

LYDIA: Yes, I suppose we have. I didn't know I had so much to say.

ST JOHN: Me either. *(He tentatively puts his hand on hers.)* Lydia?

LYDIA: Yes?

ST JOHN: I've had a wonderful time tonight.

LYDIA: Thank you, St John. So have I.

ST JOHN: And I would very much like to see you again.

LYDIA: Well, I'll see you in the morning...

ST JOHN: No, I mean **see** you, see you.

LYDIA: Date, you mean?

ST JOHN: Yes.

LYDIA: Well, yes...yes, I'd like that.

ST JOHN: Really?

LYDIA: Very much so.

ACT TWO   39

*(*LYDIA *and* ST JOHN *look into each other's eyes, then lean over the table for a kiss. As before, when their lips touch they both pull back, surprised.)*

ST JOHN: Oh…

LYDIA: Sorry…

ST JOHN: No…I just…I'm so clumsy…

LYDIA: Nonsense.

*(*ST JOHN *kisses* LYDIA *again. This time they manage to keep their lips together for a little longer before they get squeamish.)*

ST JOHN: Well…

LYDIA: Yes…

ST JOHN: *(Standing)* I suppose I should get going…it's rather late.

LYDIA: *(Standing)* Yes…busy day tomorrow….

ST JOHN: And it's your birthday…

LYDIA: Oh, right.

ST JOHN: Well…

LYDIA: Um…

ST JOHN: *(Moving closer to her)* Well, thanks again for a lovely evening.

LYDIA: Thank you.

ST JOHN: And thank Limer again for me…

*(*LYDIA *pulls* ST JOHN *to her and kisses him passionately. It doesn't quite work, but they're getting better at it.)*

LYDIA: Sorry…

ST JOHN: No…I…well…goodnight, Lydia.

LYDIA: Goodnight, St John. Sleep well.

*(*ST JOHN *exits.* LYDIA *stands, obviously wrestling with some passions that are emerging.* LIMER *enters unnoticed.)*

LYDIA: Oh, goodness. I certainly wish Charlie and Monika were here now.

LIMER: *I'm* here.

LYDIA: *(Turning)* Pardon?

LIMER: I'm here if you need anything.

LYDIA: Thank you, Limer. I'm fine.

LIMER: I thought I might give you your birthday present early, Miss.

LYDIA: You got me a present?

LIMER: Don't I always?

LYDIA: Oh, yes. Yes, you do. Thank you, Limer.

LIMER: You're welcome. Would you like your present, now?

LYDIA: If you'd like me to open it now.

LIMER: I would, Miss.

LYDIA: All right.

LIMER: *(Exiting)* Close your eyes, Miss, and don't open them until I tell you.

LYDIA: All right.

(As LIMER goes on and off stage during this next, it sings the "Happy Birthday Song." It enters pushing a gurney— there is a body under a sheet and a bow on top of the sheet. It exits, then returns with a second gurney just like the first.)

LIMER: You may open your eyes now, Miss.

LYDIA: Goodness, such large presents! Whatever can they be?

LIMER: Open this one first, Miss.

(LYDIA pulls back the sheet to reveal CHARLIE, fully dressed in his funeral suit.)

LYDIA: Oh my God! Limer, where did you get him?!

LIMER: Open the other one.

(LYDIA *pulls back the sheet to reveal* MONIKA, *dressed in her funeral dress.*)

LYDIA: Limer! What on earth have you done?

LIMER: (*Very pleased with itself*) Happy birthday, Miss!

LYDIA: Limer, these two should have been buried this afternoon! What in the hell are they doing here?

LIMER: I arranged it with the grave diggers. Old family friends.

LYDIA: Limer, that's illegal!

LIMER: Who's to know? The families saw the coffins lowered into the ground today. They didn't know they were empty.

LYDIA: I don't believe this.

LIMER: Don't you like your present?

LYDIA: Limer, they are supposed to be buried!

LIMER: But they're so pretty. It seemed like such a waste. And you were so upset when Mac took them away.

LYDIA: But we can't just keep bodies!

LIMER: I thought you'd like it.

LYDIA: Limer, it was sweet of you to think of me, but… but…they don't belong to us.

LIMER: Well, the families weren't going to keep them. They just stuck them in a hole in the ground and left. Finders keepers, losers weepers.

LYDIA: Oh, God, we could get in so much trouble for this.

LIMER: Well, I wasn't planning to publish the fact that we have them.

LYDIA: But the health inspectors...they'll wonder why these old bodies are in with the new.

LIMER: But your embalming skills are so good that they'll never know how long the bodies have been here. These bodies have a good two years left in them before anyone would notice anything. And look, here's another surprise.

(LIMER *opens and shuts* MONIKA's *mouth a few times.*)

LIMER: I took out the stitches for you.

LYDIA: Oh, Limer.

LIMER: I'm sorry, Miss. I thought you'd like them. I can take them away in the morning.

LYDIA: Where would you take them?

LIMER: Back to the cemetery.

LYDIA: Limer, I'm sorry. I know you meant well, but I just wouldn't feel right about keeping them. I would feel like I'd lied to the families. My reputation—

LIMER: You won't take anything I have to offer.

LYDIA: Stop it, Limer! I told you I appreciated the thought, but just try to understand—

LIMER: Well, I don't understand. One minute you're...

LYDIA: What?

LIMER: Nothing.

LYDIA: Say it.

LIMER: Never mind.

LYDIA: Finish the sentence, Limer.

LIMER: I just think you're fickle, that's all.

LYDIA: That will do, Limer! Go to bed. We'll talk about this in the morning.

LIMER: *(Starting to exit)* Happy birthday, Miss.

LYDIA: Thanks.

LIMER: You're welcome.

(LIMER *exits.* LYDIA *looks around, nervously She covers* CHARLIE'*s face with the sheet, then uncovers it, covers, uncovers—she can't resist looking at him. She smoothes his hair, adjusts his tie, then loosens the tie, then takes her hands away from him guiltily.)*

LYDIA: No. No, I can't, Charlie. It would be so disrespectful.

(LYDIA *glances as* MONIKA, *then goes to her.)*

LYDIA: What a beautiful dress, Monika. You look stunning.

(LYDIA *touches* MONIKA.)

LYDIA: Absolutely ravishing.

(LYDIA *opens and closes* MONIKA'*s mouth a few times.)*

LYDIA: Temptress! No. No, I can't....I...can't...I...

(LYDIA *kisses* MONIKA.)

LYDIA: God, I missed you. And you too, Charlie.

(LYDIA *goes to* CHARLIE *and kisses him.)*

LYDIA: I had a date with a man this evening, Charlie. A live one. And I had a lovely time. That's the first time I've had a date that was even remotely pleasant. I feel as if I've known him for years. You know him, Charlie. It's St John. I had a date with St John. What do you think of him? Don't you thinks he's handsome? What about you, Monika? Don't you think he's handsome? Not as handsome as Charlie, of course, but very sweet.

(LYDIA *starts loosening* CHARLIE'*s tie, unbuttoning his shirt, etc…)*

LYDIA: No one's quite as handsome as you are, Charlie. No, indeed. You are probably the most perfect specimen I have ever seen. I'm still amazed at my good fortune. You would never have given me the time of day while you were alive, but now...now you'll give me anything I want.

(LYDIA *caresses* CHARLIE *more urgently.*)

LYDIA: Anything at all. Both of you.

(LYDIA *kisses* CHARLIE *passionately.*)

(*Blackout*)

Scene Two

(*At rise, a disheveled* LYDIA *is redressing* CHARLIE. MONIKA *is also looking a bit rumpled.* LIMER *enters.*)

LIMER: Good morning, Miss. Need help?

LYDIA: No. I was just making sure they looked...

LIMER: ...like nothing happened?

LYDIA: Limer.

LIMER: (*Starting to straighten up* MONIKA) I don't see why you won't keep them. You obviously want to.

LYDIA: I can't. It wouldn't be right. Besides, what would St John say?

LIMER: Who cares?

LYDIA: Well...

LIMER: Yes, I see. You care.

LYDIA: Not really...it's just that keeping bodies past their funeral date is ethically questionable.

LIMER: I doubt he'll turn you in. Or **on**.

LYDIA: What?

LIMER: I said I doubt he will turn you in to the health inspector.

LYDIA: No, probably not, but...

LIMER: You're worried what he'll think of you.

LYDIA: No.

LIMER: Yes.

LYDIA: Is there anything wrong with that? With caring what someone thinks of you?

LIMER: It's unusual in your case, Miss, if you don't mind my saying so.

LYDIA: Well, I do mind you saying so. I have feelings, you know. I'm actually a very sensitive person. Just because I work with the dead doesn't mean **I'm** dead.

LIMER: Exactly, Miss.

(Pause. LYDIA stares at LIMER.)

LYDIA: Limer, what on earth is the matter with you lately?

LIMER: *(Whipping the sheet over MONIKA's head)* Well, since you're so sensitive, I'm sure you'll figure it out eventually. Your breakfast is ready.

(LIMER turns and exits quickly. LYDIA is angry; she roughly does up CHARLIE's tie and pulls the sheet over his face, then wheels the gurney over beside MONIKA's. ST JOHN enters.)

ST JOHN: New bodies?

LYDIA: *(She turns, startled.)* What?

ST JOHN: When did they come in?

LYDIA: Who?

ST JOHN: The new bodies.

LYDIA: These?

ST JOHN: Yes, Lydia. Those two bodies right there.

LYDIA: Last night. After you left.

ST JOHN: Let's have a look.

LYDIA: No. I'd rather you didn't.

ST JOHN: Why not?

LYDIA: I'd just rather you didn't, that's all…

ST JOHN: Oh, come, now Lydia. I won't steal them. Good-looking are they? *(He lifts the sheet off of* CHARLIE.*)* Oh my God!

LYDIA: I asked you not to look, St John.

ST JOHN: *(He lifts the sheet off of* MONIKA.*)* Oh my God! Where in the hell did they come from? I thought they were buried yesterday.

LYDIA: It was a birthday present from Limer. I've told it to return them to the cemetery.

ST JOHN: Good Lord. A birthday present?

LYDIA: I'm afraid so.

ST JOHN: I wish someone would give **me** birthday presents like these.

LYDIA: Yes. Well, anyway…I can't keep them.

ST JOHN: I suppose not.

LYDIA: Ethically it just wouldn't be…

ST JOHN: Proper…

LYDIA: Exactly.

ST JOHN: Too bad.

LYDIA: St John!

ST JOHN: It just seems like such a waste. They're so pretty.

LYDIA: You sound like Limer.

ST JOHN: *(He looks* CHARLIE *over.)* Is it upset that you want to give them back?

LYDIA: Yes. It's been very short with me lately and I'm afraid this has made things worse. I can't imagine what's got into it.

ST JOHN: It probably feels over-worked—hey, you put his finger back on.

(ST JOHN *holds up one of* CHARLIE's *hands. One of the fingers has a piece of tape around it; the end of the finger looks a bit chewed up.*)

LYDIA: Limer did that.

ST JOHN: Looks better with all of his fingers. My, my, Monika looks stunning in that dress.

LYDIA: Doesn't she though?

ST JOHN: Limer did a wonderful job on her hair and make-up.

LYDIA: Mmm. And did you ever see such beautiful bone structure?

(LYDIA *and* ST JOHN *both move in closer to* MONIKA *and touch her as they speak; it's almost a territorial struggle.*)

ST JOHN: It's perfect.

LYDIA: And her figure…

ST JOHN: Oh, don't get me started on her figure.

LYDIA: It's perfect.

ST JOHN: Absolutely perfect.

(*Pause.* LYDIA *and* ST JOHN *look at one another. They're both getting turned on.*)

ST JOHN: You know, you mustn't be cross with Limer. It was a sweet thing to do. It must care about you a lot.

LYDIA: I suppose so. (*She giggles.*)

ST JOHN: What?

LYDIA: Look what else it did.

(LYDIA *opens and closes* MONIKA's *mouth a few times.*)

ST JOHN: Awww. That's very thoughtful.

LYDIA: It is, isn't it? I shouldn't have gotten upset with it, but I was caught off guard.

(LYDIA *and* ST JOHN *stand silently stroking* MONIKA *for a moment.*)

ST JOHN: It's a shame you have to take them back.

LYDIA: Yes.

ST JOHN: It's somehow comforting have two such perfect specimens here—it sort of reminds you of the good things in life.

LYDIA: It's cheering.

ST JOHN: Yes.

(LYDIA *and* ST JOHN *are stroking* MONIKA *more urgently now. They stop, turn, look at one another and simultaneously lunge at one another for a kiss. They are both caught off guard when they connect. They jump back.*)

LYDIA: Whoops.

ST JOHN: Sorry…

LYDIA: No…it was…

ST JOHN: Here…

(ST JOHN *holds* LYDIA *very still by pinning her arms at her side; she doesn't resist. He kisses her for a long time. She doesn't move a muscle. He releases her.*)

ST JOHN: Oh, my…

LYDIA: Whew…

ST JOHN: Yes, that was…

LYDIA: Did you feel…?

ST JOHN: Yes.

(*It's* LYDIA'*s turn. She pins* ST JOHN'*s arms and kisses him passionately. He does not move.* LIMER *enters during this. It watches them kiss. It's upset.*)

LIMER: The rats ate your breakfast, Miss.

(LIMER *turns and exits before* LYDIA *has a chance to respond.*)

LYDIA: Do you see what I mean? It's gotten downright obnoxious lately.

ST JOHN: Yes.

LYDIA: It's infuriating.

ST JOHN: I'm sure it's just upset about the birthday present.

LYDIA: I was probably very abrupt with it about it.

ST JOHN: Maybe you should…no…

LYDIA: What?

ST JOHN: Nothing.

LYDIA: Keep them? Is that what you're thinking?

ST JOHN: Just for a little while. Just to make Limer happy.

LYDIA: I suppose that might cheer it up.

ST JOHN: Oh, I'm sure it would.

LYDIA: We'd have to be careful about the inspectors.

ST JOHN: We'd have to get those funeral clothes off them.

LYDIA: Of course.

ST JOHN: Well, if we're all in this together, I don't see how the inspector would know anything. He doesn't come by that often.

LYDIA: True. (*She giggles.*) I feel like a schoolgirl sneaking a piece of candy.

ST JOHN: Me too.

LYDIA: I must tell Limer. It'll be pleased that we're keeping them. Limer!

(LIMER *steps out immediately as if it's been there all along.*)

LIMER: Yes, Miss?

LYDIA: We've decided to keep Charlie and Monika—at least for a little while.

LIMER: "We"?

LYDIA: *I.* I have decided to keep them.

LIMER: Perhaps you don't need to keep them now, seeing as how you and…

LYDIA: That will do, Limer! I thought you'd be pleased.

LIMER: I couldn't be happier, Miss.

LYDIA: Good.

LIMER: Not even if you'd stabbed me in the heart with a trocar.

LYDIA: What?

LIMER: I would rather be stabbed with a trocar than to have you reject the present.

ST JOHN: It was a very thoughtful gift, Limer.

LIMER: It wasn't meant for you.

LYDIA: Limer!

ST JOHN: I know it wasn't meant for me, I was simply saying—

LIMER: I heard you.

LYDIA: Really, Limer. Your behavior is appalling lately.

LIMER: Thank you, Miss. Shall I make you another breakfast?

LYDIA: No thank you, that will be all.

LIMER: Of course it will.

LYDIA: What?

LIMER: Nothing. (*It exits.*)

LYDIA: Oooo, it makes me so mad sometimes!

ST JOHN: Don't let it get to you. You should have a nice day, it's your birthday.

LYDIA: I don't have much use for birthdays anymore. I always spend them alone, or with Limer.

ST JOHN: But today you have me. We should do something special.

LYDIA: Like what?

ST JOHN: I don't know. We could go out...

LYDIA: No.

ST JOHN: No. We could just have a nice evening together. Just the two of us. Or...

LYDIA: Or what?

ST JOHN: Never mind.

LYDIA: What?

ST JOHN: No. I'm embarrassed I thought of it.

LYDIA: Tell me, St John.

ST JOHN: No, I couldn't.

LYDIA: St John! Tell me what you were going to say.

ST JOHN: Well...we could have a nice evening...you know...the *four* of us.

LYDIA: Four?...oh, I see.

ST JOHN: Forget it. It was a dumb idea. It was impolite of me to proposition you like that.

LYDIA: I've never been propositioned, so I wouldn't worry about being impolite...in fact I've never...

ST JOHN: Never?

LYDIA: Well, in a manner of speaking, I've never...you know...

ST JOHN: Me neither.

LYDIA: Really?

ST JOHN: I've only had one date in my life.

LYDIA: Well, now you've had two, counting me.

ST JOHN: I was counting you.

LYDIA: Oh. I see.

ST JOHN: I've never met anyone like you before and I would really like to...

LYDIA: Me too. Oh, heavens, this is all happening so fast. I think.

ST JOHN: Well, we don't have to...I mean...we can go slower. Is that what people do?

LYDIA: I don't know. I think so.

ST JOHN: We can do that....just slow down.

LYDIA: I don't know if I want to slow down, though.

ST JOHN: I don't.

LYDIA: Then let's not.

ST JOHN: Okay.

(LYDIA *and* ST JOHN *rush toward one another, for a kiss. Actually, they both just stand with arms down at their sides and press their lips together without moving. They hold the lip lock for quite sometime.*)

ST JOHN: Oh, God, Lydia...I've never felt so...so...

LYDIA: Alive.

(LYDIA *and* ST JOHN *lock lips again, as the lights fade.*)

(*Blackout*)

Scene Three

(LYDIA is alone, pulling off CHARLIE's funeral suit. LIMER enters and watches her for a moment, then walks up behind her and stands very close to her. When she senses the presence, she turns and is face to face with it.)

LIMER: Hello, Miss.

LYDIA: Mother of God, Limer. Will you stop that!

LIMER: Beg pardon, Miss.

LYDIA: You do that deliberately, don't you?

LIMER: Not at all, Miss.

LYDIA: No, I think you really enjoy frightening me.

LIMER: Honestly, I don't. I don't mean to scare you.

LYDIA: Then why do you insist on creeping in like that?

LIMER: I like to watch you.

LYDIA: What?

LIMER: You wouldn't understand.

LYDIA: Probably not.

(Pause. LYDIA returns to undressing CHARLIE. LIMER starts on MONIKA. They do this in silence for a while.)

LIMER: Where's your saint?

LYDIA: St John's gone to the morgue with Mac.

LIMER: Good.

LYDIA: You don't like him, do you Limer?

LIMER: No, miss.

LYDIA: Why not?

(LIMER shrugs.)

LYDIA: He's perfectly nice.

LIMER: Yes, Miss.

LYDIA: So why don't you like him?

LIMER: I don't like his presence. I don't like him being here…with us.

LYDIA: Well, we need his help right now whether you like it or not.

LIMER: I didn't think it would turn out like this.

LYDIA: What?

LIMER: The fire. I thought we'd get better looking bodies after the fire. I didn't think we'd get *him*.

(LYDIA *looks at* LIMER. *Their gazes lock.*)

LYDIA: What's that supposed to mean?

LIMER: What would you like it to mean?

LYDIA: Are you saying what I think you're saying?

LIMER: What's that, Miss?

LYDIA: Are you saying that *you* started that fire?

LIMER: I'm not saying that at all, Miss.

LYDIA: Limer—

LIMER: Why on earth would anyone want to burn down a mortuary, Miss? It was probably an accident. Faulty heating system or something, don't you think?

(LYDIA *doesn't answer.*)

LIMER: Or perhaps the saint was trying to make a T V dinner, or some such delicacy, and the kitchen caught fire. Most likely it was bad wiring, though. I've read that's the usual cause of fires.

LYDIA: *(Not quite believing it)* Limer…

(LYDIA *starts to say something,* LIMER *looks at her. She thinks better of it and remains silent. Pause. They continue working on the bodies.*)

LIMER: I'm glad you're keeping your presents, Miss.

LYDIA: I'm sorry I was so short with you about them.

LIMER: Apology accepted.

LYDIA: I like them, really I do. It's good to see them again.

LIMER: Do you like them better than you like **him**?

LYDIA: Who?

LIMER: The saint.

LYDIA: St John. I don't know. It's different with him.

LIMER: Better?

LYDIA: Different. It takes getting used to, you know, being with…

LIMER: I understand.

LYDIA: Do you?

LIMER: *(Indicating* CHARLIE *and* MONIKA*)* Well, not *this*. But I understand you. No need to be embarrassed, Miss. To each its own. A leopard can't change its spots and all that…

LYDIA: It's just that when I was growing up here—

LIMER: Enough said. You don't need to explain anything to me. You should know that by now, at least.

LYDIA: I don't know much of anything, Limer. I'm not very good with people.

LIMER: I know.

(LYDIA *pulls the sheet over* CHARLIE's *head.* LIMER *pulls the sheet over* MONIKA's *head.)*

May I have the rest of the day off, Miss?

LYDIA: Of course.

LIMER: I need to do some things.

LYDIA: Certainly.

LIMER: I've made you and your saint a casserole for this evening—the heating instructions are on it. Your birthday cake is in the pantry.

LYDIA: Thank you. That was very thoughtful.

LIMER: You're welcome.

LYDIA: Well, have a good day.

LIMER: Miss?

LYDIA: Yes?

LIMER: May I touch you?

LYDIA: What do you mean?

LIMER: I just want to touch your face. I work all day long with the faces of the dead and sometimes I need to touch something living.

LYDIA: I understand.

LIMER: Do you?

LYDIA: No.

LIMER: I know. May I?

LYDIA: All right.

(LIMER *reaches out and strokes* LYDIA's *face.*)

LIMER: Thank you.

LYDIA: You're welcome.

LIMER: I'll put away their clothes before I go.

LYDIA: Thanks.

LIMER: Happy Birthday, Miss.

LYDIA: See you in the morning.

LIMER: Yes.

(LYDIA *exits.* LIMER *picks up* CHARLIE's *and* MONIKA's *clothes. The lights fade…*)

(*Blackout*)

Scene Four

(The lights come up on four bodies lying together under sheets—several gurneys have been put together to make one big "bed." CHARLIE has an "erection." LYDIA and ST JOHN are lying between CHARLIE and MONIKA, they are asleep. LYDIA rolls over in her sleep. ST JOHN starts awake, thus waking LYDIA who also jumps.)

ST JOHN: Heavens, I don't even remember falling asleep.

LYDIA: It was right after you and Monika...um...

ST JOHN: Oh, right. Listen, Lydia, do you want to talk about it?

LYDIA: No.

ST JOHN: Do you...do you want to try again?

LYDIA: I don't know.

ST JOHN: Perhaps if you wouldn't ...

LYDIA: Wouldn't what?

ST JOHN: Well, perhaps if you wouldn't **move**...quite so much...

LYDIA: I could ask the same of you.

ST JOHN: Yes, I suppose you could.

LYDIA: I don't know if this is going to work, St John.

ST JOHN: I want it to work. I really do. I think we just need some practice is all.

LYDIA: Perhaps.

(ST JOHN leans over and kisses LYDIA and pushes her down and holds her still and becomes more passionate. She reaches up an arm and puts it around his neck. He jumps back.)

LYDIA: Oh, sorry...

ST JOHN: That's okay.

LYDIA: Perhaps if you tied me down.

ST JOHN: No, I couldn't do that.

LYDIA: Lie down.

ST JOHN: What?

LYDIA: Lie down and don't move.

(ST JOHN obeys.)

LYDIA: Now, just let me do all the work. Close your eyes.

ST JOHN: Okay.

LYDIA: No talking.

(LYDIA picks up ST JOHN's hand and strokes her own face and body with it. He starts to take over control of his hand, stroking on his own.)

LYDIA: Let me do it! Relax.

(LYDIA puts his hand down, then climbs on top of him, kissing him, touching him, etc... ST JOHN struggles not to react.)

LYDIA: Yes, that's good. Just relax. Don't move. Don't move a muscle.

(As LYDIA and ST JOHNy both become more and more excited, it is harder and harder for him to stay still. He automatically seizes her in his arms. She is caught off guard and screams.)

ST JOHN: Oh God.

LYDIA: Be still.

ST JOHN: No, you be still.

LYDIA: It's my turn.

ST JOHN: Look, this'll just take a sec, I'm—

LYDIA: St John, please. You're ruining it.

ST JOHN: But I...

LYDIA: Oh, never mind. *(She turns away from him.)*
Charlie!

ST JOHN: Monika!

(LYDIA lunges for CHARLIE and ST JOHN lunges for MONIKA and they take out their passions on their respective bodies as the lights fade…)

(Blackout)

Scene Five

(The next morning. The lights are dim. LYDIA is asleep. ST JOHN is putting on his clothes. There is an extra gurney in the room, which he does not notice. He kisses her lightly. She jumps up.)

ST JOHN: Shhh, shhh. It's just me.

LYDIA: Oh. What are you doing?

ST JOHN: I've got to run back to my apartment to get a clean suit for work. I'll be back before opening.

LYDIA: Oh, all right.

ST JOHN: I had a wonderful time last night.

LYDIA: We didn't do very well, did we?

ST JOHN: No. I'm sorry.

LYDIA: It's not your fault.

ST JOHN: I'm disappointed in myself.

LYDIA: I didn't think it would be so difficult.

ST JOHN: I didn't either.

LYDIA: It's not that I don't like you, St John—

ST JOHN: No need to explain.

LYDIA: All those mortician jokes…perhaps people have reason to laugh…

St John: Don't say that, Lydia. We're decent human beings—perfectly respectable people who would never harm a living thing.

Lydia: That's because we don't know any living things.

St John: I know you, and you know me.

Lydia: It's a start.

St John: Look, Lydia, no matter what happens with... with all this, you and I must remain friends. I like talking to you—it makes me feel good to talk to you. I've even laughed with you. We understand each other.

Lydia: Yes.

St John: Good. It's settled.

Lydia: What do we do now?

St John: I don't know.

Lydia: Maybe we should just talk about it later.

St John: Fine.

Lydia: Fine.

St John: I'll see you shortly. Go back to sleep.

Lydia: See you soon.

(St John *exits*. Lydia *stretches, strokes* Charlie, *then starts to curl up with him. She sees the extra gurney and is puzzled. She goes to the gurney and notices a note pinned to the sheet covering the body. She reads the note silently, then slowly puts it down, stunned. After staring at the body for a moment, she gently pulls the sheet back to reveal* Limer. *She stares at it, then reaches out to touch its face.*)

(*Blackout*)

END OF PLAY

www.ingramcontent.com/pod-product-compliance
Lightning Source LLC
Chambersburg PA
CBHW052223090426
42741CB00010B/2650

* 9 7 8 0 8 8 1 4 5 7 3 1 5 *